ORIGAMI

not-quite-so-easy
ORIGAMI

by Mary Meinking

Capstone
press®

Mankato, Minnesota

Snap Books are published by Capstone Press,

151 Good Counsel Drive, P.O. Box 669, Mankato, Minnesota 56002.

www.capstonepress.com

Library of Congress Cataloging-in-Publication Data
Meinking, Mary.

    Not-quite-so-easy origami / by Mary Meinking.

    p. cm. — (Snap books. Origami)

    Summary: "Provides step-by-step instructions for moderately easy origami models, including a
hopping frog, gliding airplane, and flapping crane" — Provided by publisher.

    Includes bibliographical references and index.

    ISBN-13: 978-1-4296-2021-5 (hardcover)

    ISBN-10: 1-4296-2021-8 (hardcover)

    1. Origami — Juvenile literature. I. Title. II. Series.
TT870.M424 2009

736'.982 — dc22   2008001679

Editor: Kathryn Clay
Designer: Bobbi J. Wyss
Photo Researcher: Dede Barton
Photo Stylist: Sarah L. Schuette
Scheduler: Marcy Morin

Photo Credits:
All principal photography in this book by Capstone Press/Karon Dubke
Capstone Press/TJ Thoraldson Digital Photography, steps (all)
Syd Spies, 32

The author would like to dedicate this book to: Scott, Britt, and Ben for your loving support and encouragement
as my writing career unfolded.

1 2 3 4 5 6 13 12 11 10 09 08

TABLE OF CONTENTS

page 8

page 20

page 26

INTRODUCTION

Ordinary paper has a secret identity just waiting to come out. With just a few folds, you can turn plain paper into something wonderful. Will it turn into an airplane, a cicada, or an envelope? Use your imagination to make just about anything out of paper.

Some origami models may seem tricky at first glance. But don't get scared off by many steps or difficult folds. Take your time to learn each step. If you get stuck, don't give up. Just back up and try again. With a little practice, you'll soon become an expert.

MATERIALS

Before you begin, take some time to choose your paper. Traditional origami paper can be found at craft stores, on the Internet, and in some bookstores. It's usually colored on one side and white on the other. But you don't have to use special origami paper. Almost any kind of paper can be used for origami. Notebook paper, newspapers, dollar bills, and wrapping paper all can be folded into fun shapes.

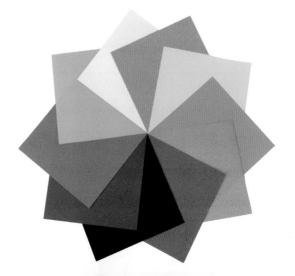

HOW TO USE THIS BOOK

Origami models are made with valley folds and mountain folds. All other folds are just combinations of these two basic folds.

Valley folds are represented by a dashed line. The paper is creased along the line as the top surface of the paper is folded against itself like a book.

Mountain folds are represented by a pink dashed and dotted line. The paper is creased along the line and folded behind.

Reverse folds are made by opening a pocket slightly and folding the model inside itself along existing creases.

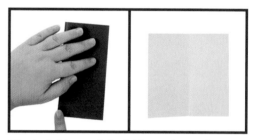

Mark folds are light folds used to make reference creases for a later step. Ideally, a mark fold will not be seen in the finished model.

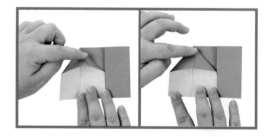

Squash folds are formed by lifting one edge of a pocket and reforming it so the spine gets flattened. The existing creases become new edges.

FOLDING SYMBOLS

A crease from a previous step.	Fold the paper in the direction of the arrow.
A fold or edge hidden under another layer of paper; also used as an imaginary extension of an existing line.	Fold the paper and then unfold it.
Turn the paper over or rotate it to a new position.	Fold the paper behind.

FOLDING 101: HOW TO MAKE A SQUARE

Most origami models are made from square sheets of paper. If you don't have square origami paper, don't worry. It's easy to make your own from any size paper. Here's how:

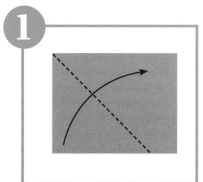

Fold the bottom left corner to the top edge.

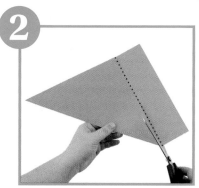

Cut off the extra strip of paper.

A finished square.

TRAPDOOR ENVELOPE

Based on a model by Jeremy Shafer

Pass out party invitations in this envelope, and you're sure to get a response. Have your friends pull on the tab. They'll be surprised to see the envelope burst open and the contents spill out.

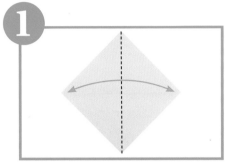

1 Start with the colored side down. Valley fold in half and unfold.

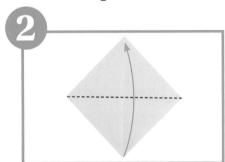

2 Valley fold in half.

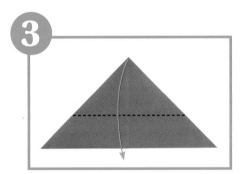

3 Valley fold the top layer past the bottom edge.

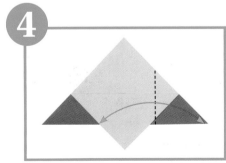

4 Valley fold to the left edge and unfold.

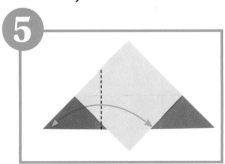

5 Repeat step 4 on the left side.

6 Tuck the left triangle inside the pocket of the right triangle.

7 Valley fold slightly past the envelope's opening.

8 Finished envelope.

You are Invited!

...in celebrating Jenn...
...ting at th...

9

BOOKMARK

Traditional Model

Mark your spot in style with this easy-to-make bookmark. You'll never have to worry about losing your place again. These homemade bookmarks also make great gifts for your favorite reader.

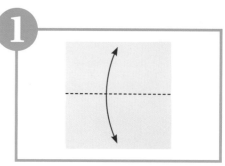

Start with the colored side down.
Valley fold in half and unfold.

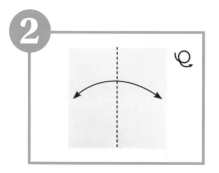

Valley fold in half and unfold.
Rotate the paper.

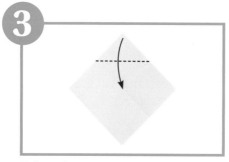

Valley fold to the center crease.

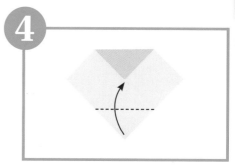

Valley fold to the center crease.

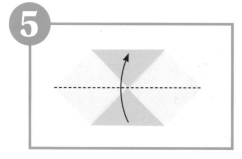

Valley fold in half.

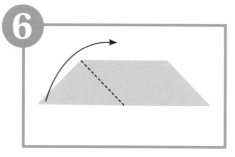

Valley fold along the center crease.

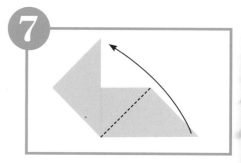

Repeat step 6 on the right side.

8

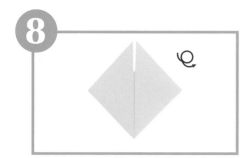

Turn the paper over.

9

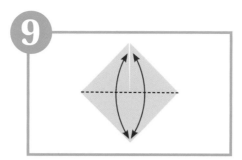

Valley fold both triangle points down and unfold.

10

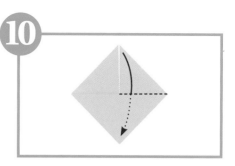

Tuck the top right point into the front pocket.

11

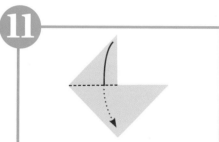

Repeat step 10 on the left side.

12

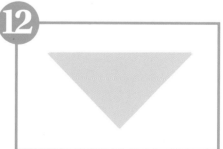

Finished bookmark.

GLIDING AIRPLANE

Traditional Model

You've probably made a paper airplane before. But did you know you were also making origami? Fold a few of these and challenge your friends to a paper airplane contest. The plane that flies the farthest wins.

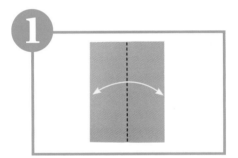

Start with a rectangular sheet of paper. Valley fold in half and unfold.

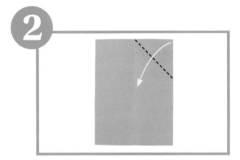

Valley fold to the center crease.

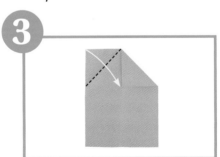

Repeat step 2 on the left side.

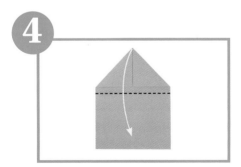

Valley fold 1 inch (2.54 centimeters) from the bottom of the paper.

5

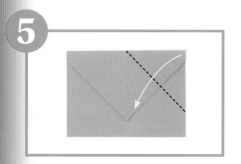

Valley fold to the center crease.

6

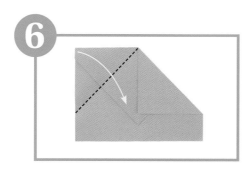

Repeat step 5 on the left side.

7

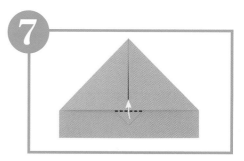

Valley fold the mini triangle.

8

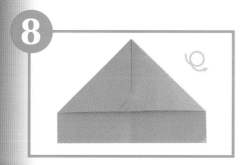

Turn the paper over and rotate.

9

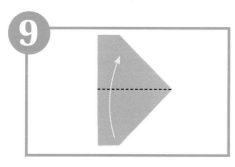

Valley fold in half.

10

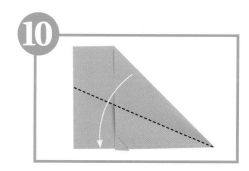

Valley fold the top layer along the bottom edge.

11

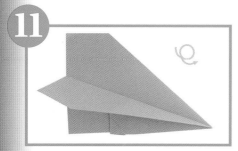

Turn the paper over.

12

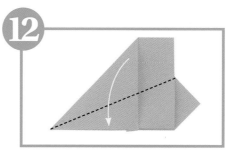

Valley fold along the bottom edge.

13

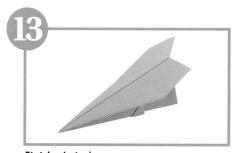

Finished airplane.

SOMERSAULT SQUARE

Based on a model by Seiro Takekawa

While this model may not look like an acrobat, it sure acts like one. Give it a tap and watch it somersault across a table.

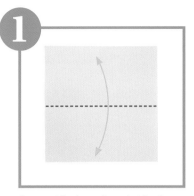

1 Start with the colored side down. Valley fold in half and unfold.

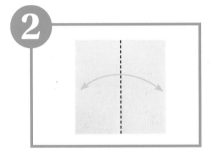

2 Valley fold in half and unfold.

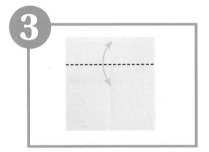

3 Valley fold to the crease made in step 1 and unfold.

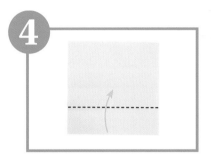

4 Valley fold to the crease made in step 1.

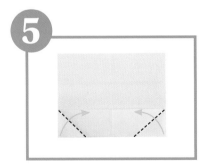

5 Valley fold to the crease made in step 1.

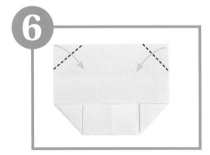

6 Valley fold to the crease made in step 3.

7 Valley fold to the crease made in step 3.

8

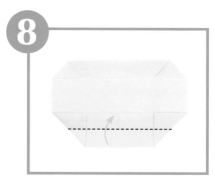

Valley fold to the center crease.

9

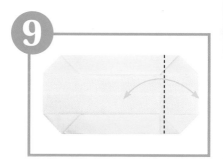

Valley fold to the center crease.
Unfold halfway.

10

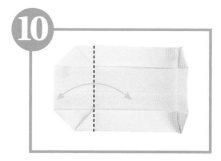

Repeat step 9 on the left side.

11

Finished somersault square. Make sure the thicker side is on top before using.

Somersault Show

Line up a few somersault squares in a row. Tap the first one over. Watch it knock down the other squares like dominoes.

15

COASTER

Traditional Model

The next time you have friends over, offer them something to drink. Come back with a tray of drinks and colorful coasters. Two sheets of double-sided paper work best for this project.

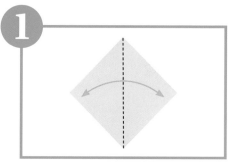

Start with the colored side down.
Valley fold in half and unfold.

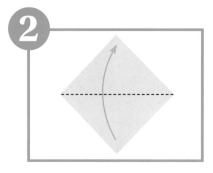

Valley fold in half.

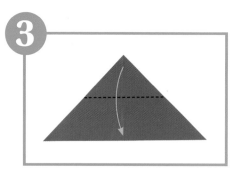

Valley fold the top layer to the bottom edge.

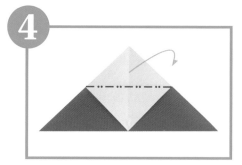

Mountain fold the top corner to the bottom edge.

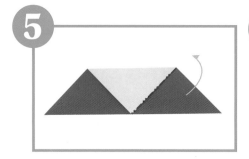

Mountain fold to the center crease.

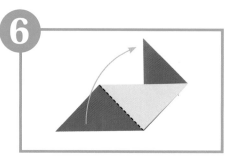

Valley fold to the center crease.

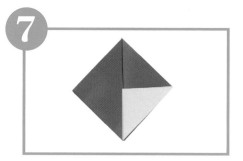

Repeat steps 1 through 6 with another sheet of paper.

8

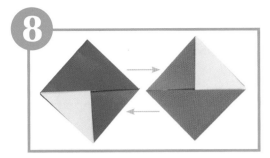

Place the models side-by-side, with the loose triangles facing each other. Slide the models together.

9

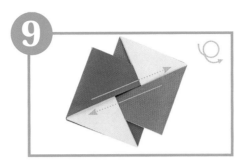

Turn the model over. Tuck the top triangles into the pockets.

10

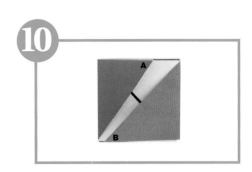

Tuck points A and B into the pockets.

11

Push the two pieces together to make a snug fit.

12

Finished coaster.

PINE TREE

Traditional Model

Get lost in a forest of origami trees. Make several trees in different shades of green paper. Change the trunk lengths to create trees that are different shapes and sizes.

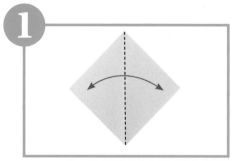

1 Start with the colored side down. Valley fold in half and unfold.

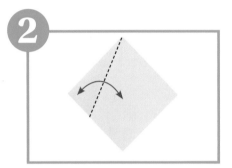

2 Valley fold to the center crease and unfold.

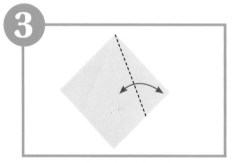

3 Repeat step 2 on the right side.

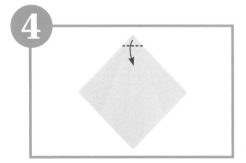

4 Valley fold the top corner down slightly.

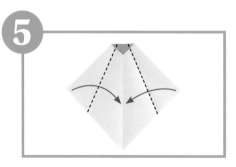

5 Valley fold on the existing creases.

18

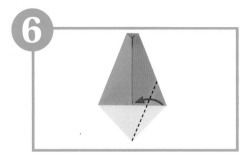

6

Valley fold to the center crease.

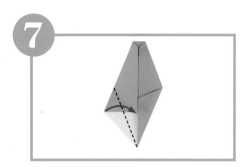

7

Repeat step 6 on the left side.

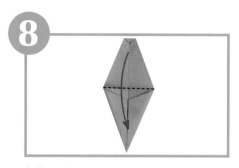

8

Valley fold.

9

Valley fold the top layer up past the top edge to create the trunk. Tuck the trunk under the flaps beneath it.

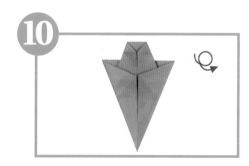

10

Turn the paper over and rotate.

Origami Ornaments
These mini pine trees make great holiday decorations. Punch a hole in the tops and use string to hang them as ornaments.

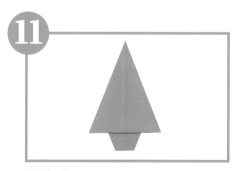

11

Finished pine tree.

CICADA

Traditional Model

The cicada origami model has been folded for centuries. In many Asian cultures, these insects are symbols of good fortune. Make your own origami cicada for a good luck charm.

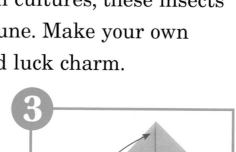

1 Start with the colored side down. Valley fold the paper in half.

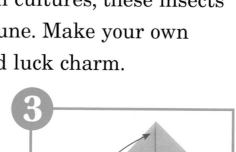

2 Valley fold to the point.

3 Repeat step 2 on the left side.

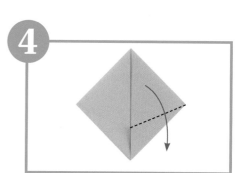

4 Valley fold the top tip down.

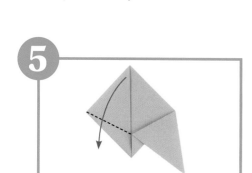

5 Repeat step 4 on the left side.

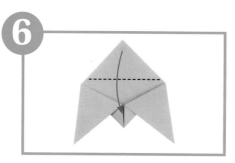

6 Valley fold the top layer. Leave part of the tail showing.

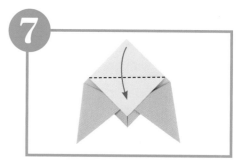

7 Valley fold. Leave part of the white edge showing.

8

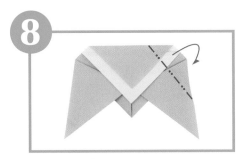

Mountain fold.

9

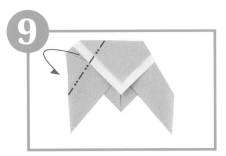

Repeat step 8 on the left side.

10

Valley fold to create an eye.

11

Repeat step 10 on the left side.

12

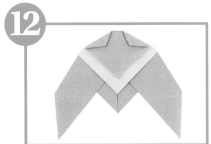

Finished cicada.

HOPPING FROG

Traditional Model

Did you know you can play origami leapfrog? To make this model, you will need a rectangular sheet of paper. This model works best if made from stiff paper, such as a recipe card or construction paper.

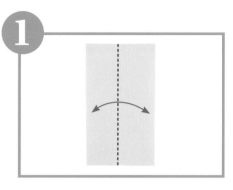

1

Start with the white side up. Valley fold in half and unfold.

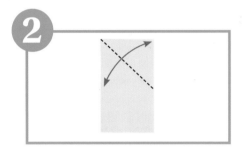

2

Valley fold to meet the left edge and unfold.

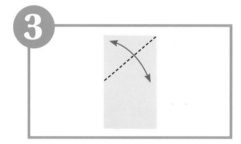

3

Valley fold to meet the right edge and unfold.

4

Turn the paper over.

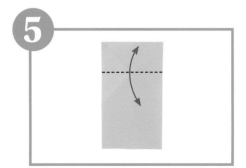

5

Valley fold to meet the edge of the crease and unfold.

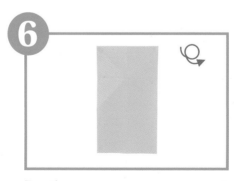

6

Turn the paper over.

7

Squash fold using the creases formed in steps 2 through 5.

8

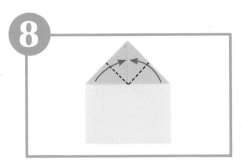

Valley fold to the center crease.

9

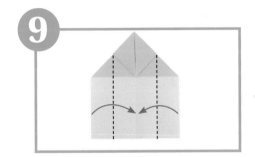

Valley fold to the center crease.

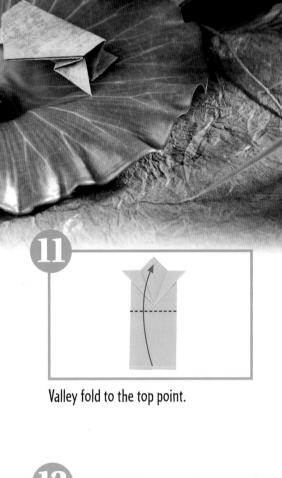

10

Valley fold the top triangles outward.

11

Valley fold to the top point.

12

Valley fold to the bottom edge. Then turn the model over.

13

Finished frog.

23

PINWHEEL

Traditional Model

Making a pinwheel is fun and easy. It's no wonder they've been popular toys for more than 100 years. A pinwheel spins by blowing on it. Out of breath? Let the wind do the work for you.

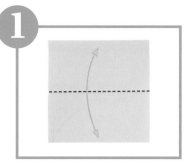

1

Start with the colored side down.
Valley fold in half and unfold.

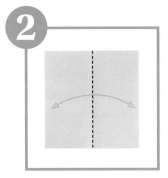

2

Valley fold in half and unfold.

3

Turn the paper over.

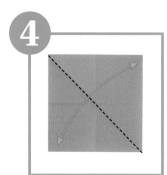

4

Valley fold in half and unfold.

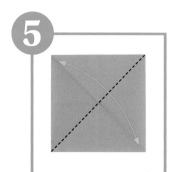

5

Valley fold in half and unfold.

6

Turn the paper over.

7

Valley fold to the center crease.

8

Repeat step 7 on the left side.

9

Valley fold corners to the center crease and unfold.

24

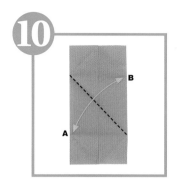

10 Valley fold point A to point B and unfold.

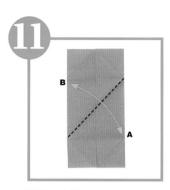

11 Valley fold point A to point B and unfold.

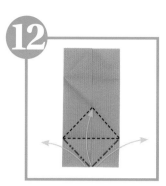

12 Valley fold bottom edge to the center. Allow the side triangles to squash fold out to the sides.

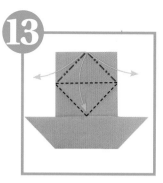

13 Repeat step 12 on the top.

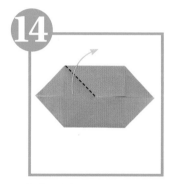

14 Valley fold to the center crease.

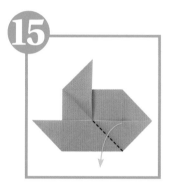

15 Valley fold to the center crease.

16 Finished pinwheel.

How to Use

To create the pinwheels shown below, use a pushpin to stick the pinwheel onto a straw. Blow on the pinwheel and watch it spin.

FLAPPING CRANE

Traditional Model

The traditional paper crane is perhaps the most popular origami model. This version of the paper crane flaps its wings. Just pull on the tail to see it fly.

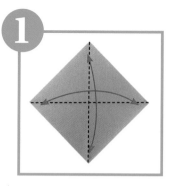

1

Start with the colored side up.
Valley fold in half both ways and unfold.

2

Turn the paper over.

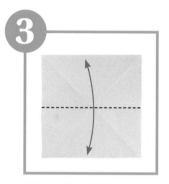

3

Valley fold in half and unfold.

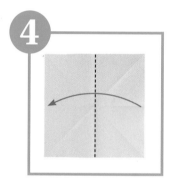

4

Valley fold in half.

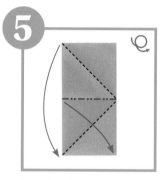

5

Squash fold and rotate.

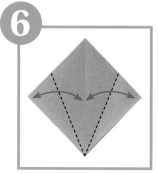

6

Valley fold the top layer to the center crease and unfold.

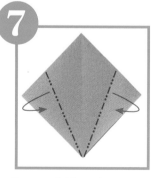

7

Reverse fold on the creases formed in step 6.

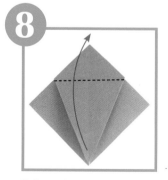

8

Valley fold the point up.

9

Turn the paper over.

26

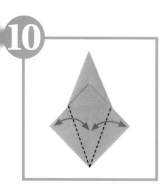

10 Repeat steps 6 through 8.

11 Valley fold and unfold.

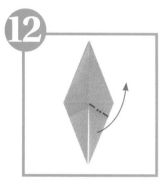

12 Reverse fold along the crease formed in step 11.

13 Repeat step 12 on the left side.

14 Reverse fold to create the crane's head.

15 Gently bend down the wings.

16 Finished crane.

Fly, Fly Birdie

Watch this bird try to fly away. Hold on to the point just below the bird's head. Gently tug on the tail to make the wings flap.

FUN FACTS

The world's smallest origami model was of the pajarita bird. In 1993, Lluis Valldeneu i Bigas, a Spanish watchmaker, folded the bird out of paper measuring just over one hundredth of an inch (0.3 millimeters) on each side. He used two pairs of tweezers and a magnifying glass to accomplish this tiny task. The finished bird was the size of the period at the end of this sentence.

World Origami Days is celebrated October 24 through November 11. American origami pioneer Lillian Oppenheimer's birthday is on October 24. November 11 is Japan's traditional Origami Day. During this time, people around the world fold origami models and teach others their techniques.

On October 23, 2004, Akie Morita broke a world record by folding 100 paper cranes in just 98 minutes.

In 1955, 11-year-old Sadako Sasaki developed a type of cancer called leukemia. Sadako knew of a legend that said anyone who folded 1,000 paper cranes would be granted a wish. She went to work folding cranes so she could wish to get well. But she was too ill and died after making only 645 cranes. Her classmates finished the remaining 355 cranes. A statue of Sadako holding a paper crane stands in Hiroshima's Peace Park.

WHAT'S NEXT. . .

You've practiced your folding skills on all of the projects in this book. Are you ready to try some more difficult projects? Then check out the next book in this series. *Sort-of-Difficult Origami* will put your skills to the test.

In this book, you'll learn how to make tulips, penguins, seals, and more. New folds are introduced, and the projects have more steps. The models are challenging, but your practice will pay off.

GLOSSARY

acrobat (AK-ruh-bat) — a person who performs gymnastics acts that require great skill

cicada (si-CAY-duh) — a type of insect that looks like a giant fly

crease (KREESE) — to make lines or folds in something

leukemia (loo-KEE-mee-uh) — a form of cancer that affects blood cells

ornament (OR-nuh-muhnt) — a small, attractive object used for decorating

rotate (ROH-tate) — to turn around or put in a different position

somersault (SUHM-ur-sawlt) — a gymnastics move where you tuck your head into your chest and roll in a circle

READ MORE

Alexander, Chris. *Sort-of-Difficult Origami.* Origami. Mankato, Minn.: Capstone Press, 2009.

Berry, Thiranut Deborah. *Origami for Fun!* For Fun! Minneapolis: Compass Point Books, 2006.

Krier, Ann Kristen. *Totally Cool Origami Animals.* New York: Sterling, 2007.

INTERNET SITES

FactHound offers a safe, fun way to find Internet sites related to this book. All of the sites on FactHound have been researched by our staff.

Here's how:
1. Visit *www.facthound.com*
2. Choose your grade level.
3. Type in this book ID **1429620218** for age-appropriate sites. You may also browse subjects by clicking on letters, or by clicking on pictures and words.
4. Click on the **Fetch It** button.

FactHound will fetch the best sites for you!

ABOUT THE AUTHOR

Mary Meinking grew up creating arts and crafts with her mother and two younger sisters. She took art classes where she drew and painted. Mary decided to turn her hobby into a profession. She studied art at the University of Kansas and has been a graphic artist ever since.

Mary shared her love for arts and crafts with her two children. Together they enjoy folding origami and paper airplanes. Mary's been published in eleven children's magazines and wrote the book *Cash Crop to Cash Cow* (2009). She currently lives in Spirit Lake, Iowa.

INDEX